Original title:
Lunar Lullabies and Sleepy Vibes

Copyright © 2024 Creative Arts Management OÜ
All rights reserved.

Author: Helena Marchant
ISBN HARDBACK: 978-9916-90-364-3
ISBN PAPERBACK: 978-9916-90-365-0

Harbinger of Night

As the sun dips low, shadows creep,
Whispers of dusk in silence deep.
Stars awaken, twinkling bright,
They herald softly the coming night.

Cool breezes dance through rustling leaves,
Night's gentle touch, a soul it weaves.
The world transformed, a hush descends,
In the heart of darkness, magic blends.

Moonlight glimmers on the stream,
Nature's lullaby, a sweet dream.
The owl calls out, wisdom in flight,
A symphony born of the harbinger night.

The Quiet Moon's Song

In the stillness, soft and clear,
The quiet moon sings to those who hear.
Her silver beams, a calming glow,
Embrace the earth where shadows flow.

Whispers of night, in gentle rhyme,
Time slows down in this peaceful clime.
Stars lend their voices, harmonize,
Under the watch of midnight skies.

Crickets chirp a lullaby sweet,
Nature's orchestra, a perfect beat.
As dreams take flight on moonlit wings,
The night reveals the joy she brings.

Soft Starlit Reflections

Glistening points in an inky sea,
Soft starlit reflections, wild and free.
Mirrors of dreams across the lake,
In their glow, new paths we make.

A tranquil moment, hearts align,
Wishing upon stars that brightly shine.
The world feels lighter, burdens erased,
In the tapestry of night, we're embraced.

Thoughts wander freely on night's soft breath,
Each twinkle a promise, transcending death.
In silent wonder, we find the light,
As starlit reflections guide our flight.

Cradle of the Night

In the cradle of night, we find our peace,
A shroud of darkness where worries cease.
The moon hangs low, a guardian bright,
Wrapping the world in tender light.

Dreams float gently on silver streams,
Awash in whispers of moonlit dreams.
Stars are scattered like grains of sand,
In this serene place, hand in hand.

Soft murmurs weave through the velvet skies,
A lullaby cradling sleepy eyes.
Night's embrace is a sweet delight,
Life's precious moments in the cradle of night.

Nightfall's Soft Embrace

The sun dips low, the sky turns dark,
Whispers of night, a gentle spark.
Shadows stretch across the ground,
In twilight's hush, peace can be found.

Stars awaken, oh so bright,
Glistening gems in the velvet night.
The moon, a lantern, hangs above,
Casting dreams wrapped in love.

The Silence of Starlight

In the stillness, silence sings,
Through the void, a calmness clings.
Stars converse in twinkling tones,
Echoes of ancient, distant bones.

A cosmic dance, the night unfolds,
Stories of mysteries yet untold.
In this quiet, hearts align,
Bound by dreams, your hand in mine.

Tranquil Moonscapes

Underneath the silver glow,
Dreams embark, and thoughts may flow.
Mountains rise in gentle grace,
Kissed by light in a soft embrace.

Lakes reflect the tranquil skies,
Where peace is found, the spirit flies.
In stillness reigns the calming tide,
As we journey through night's wide stride.

Drifting Through the Midnight

Lost in thought, I gently glide,
Through endless darkness, I confide.
Whispers echo, sweet and low,
Guiding me where moonlight flows.

The world asleep, a slumbered dream,
Where every breath feels like a theme.
I drift along with starlit grace,
In midnight's arms, I find my place.

Midnight's Gentle Kiss

Stars twinkle softly above their glow,
The moon whispers secrets only we know.
A breeze carries dreams on its tender wing,
In this tranquil moment, our hearts take wing.

Shadows entwine in a delicate sway,
As night holds us close, it bids us to stay.
With each fleeting breath, the world fades away,
In midnight's embrace, forever we'll play.

Whispers in the Night

A soft sigh of wind through the trees,
Unfolds tales of lovers, carried with ease.
The night cloaks our hopes in a gentle embrace,
While the stars spin their dreams in celestial space.

Every shadow holds whispers of yore,
Where memories linger and souls can soar.
In the stillness, our secrets take flight,
Guided by the warmth of the soft, silver light.

Dreamweaver's Dance

Through realms of slumber, we drift and glide,
In a waltz of wishes where dreams collide.
Each step a tapestry, woven with care,
In the breath of the night, we float through the air.

Stars paint the sky with strokes of pure delight,
While we dance through the shadows, lost in the night.
With every heartbeat, our spirits entwine,
In this magical realm, your hand remains mine.

The Calm Before the Dawn

Silence blankets the world in soft hues,
As night holds its breath, preparing for news.
The horizon whispers of colors to come,
In the stillness, the heart beats like a drum.

With every fleeting second, the moment draws near,
A promise of sunlight, of warmth, and of cheer.
The stars fade away as the night wears thin,
In the calm before dawn, new journeys begin.

Restless Stars

In the night, they shimmer bright,
Flickering dreams in endless flight.
Guiding travelers across the dark,
Each glowing glint a silent spark.

Whispers of ancient tales unfold,
Written in stardust, brave and bold.
Restless hearts beneath their gaze,
Searching for hope in the cosmic haze.

Gentle Hearts

Softly beating, tender and warm,
Cradled in love, they find their charm.
In quiet moments, softly shared,
Gentle hearts know how to care.

Through storms of life, they stand as one,
Two souls entwined, their journey begun.
A dance of trust beneath the sky,
In tender whispers, they learn to fly.

The Moon's Velvet Touch

A silver glow on tranquil seas,
The moonlight dances with gentle ease.
Casting shadows, dreams take flight,
In the soft embrace of the night.

Whispers linger in the cool air,
Secrets shared with those who dare.
The velvet touch of lunar grace,
Leaves a trace on the heart's face.

Peace Beneath the Starlit Canopy

Underneath the vast expanse,
Where stars twinkle, waiting to dance.
We find our peace, a quiet bliss,
In the gentle night's tender kiss.

Nature's hush wraps us in light,
A tranquil pause in soft twilight.
Beneath this canopy, dreams arise,
Clothed in the warmth of cosmic skies.

Echoes of Celestial Stillness

In the depths of night, a calm reigns,
Echoes linger on quiet plains.
Celestial whispers touch the soul,
In stillness, hearts find their whole.

Stars align in silent praise,
Moments frozen in time's embrace.
Each twinkling light a memory,
In celestial stillness, we find the key.

Dreams Beneath the Stars

In the hush of night's sigh,
Wishes float up high,
Moonlight whispers softly,
As the world drifts by.

Tender dreams take flight,
Chasing shadows bright,
Underneath the canvas,
Of the velvet night.

Stars blink in rhythm,
With hearts that are free,
Guiding us through the dark,
To where we long to be.

In the silence we find,
A spark of delight,
Dreams beneath the stars,
Our souls in the light.

Nocturnal Harmonies

Crickets sing their tune,
Beneath the silver moon,
Nature hums a lullaby,
In the dark's cocoon.

Gentle breezes sway,
As the shadows play,
Warmth of the night wraps,
The ending of the day.

Whispers of the night,
Softly hold us tight,
In this tranquil space,
Everything feels right.

Under stars so bold,
Stories yet untold,
In nocturnal harmonies,
Our dreams unfold.

Slumber's Gentle Embrace

Waves of sleepy sighs,
Entwine like lullabies,
Cradled in the stillness,
Where peace softly lies.

Pillows hug our thoughts,
As daylight slowly rots,
In slumber's gentle arms,
Time quietly plots.

Each breath a soft song,
As we drift along,
In the arms of the night,
Where we all belong.

Wrapped in dreams and light,
Until the morning bright,
In slumber's sweet embrace,
We take our flight.

Twilight Musings

Colors bleed through the sky,
As day whispers goodbye,
Embers fade in the dusk,
With a soft, gentle sigh.

Thoughts drift like the clouds,
In the evening shrouds,
Painting dreams on the canvas,
Of darkness, wrapped in crowds.

Moments linger long,
As silence sings a song,
Twilight holds our secrets,
In its melodic throng.

Beneath the fading light,
Everything feels right,
In twilight musings,
We dance through the night.

Whispering Shadows

In the dark where whispers play,
Shadows dance, softly sway.
Moonlight drapes the silent ground,
Echoes of the night resound.

Leaves rustle with secrets untold,
As night's blanket, stars unfold.
A breeze carries hidden dreams,
Wrapped in the silence, it seems.

Figures flicker, shapes deceive,
In the twilight, we believe.
Each whisper paints a story bright,
In the embrace of the night.

Hushed tones flutter, weaving fate,
Time drifts softly, can't wait.
In shadows deep, we lose our way,
But find our hearts in the play.

Restful Radiance

Sunset spills its amber hue,
Over valleys, vast and new.
Gentle light, a calming balm,
Nature whispers, sweet and calm.

Golden rays kiss the sinking day,
While shadows stretch and fade away.
In stillness, peace begins to grow,
As stars above begin to glow.

Beneath the sky, dreams take flight,
Wrapped in the warmth of fading light.
Each moment drapes in golden grace,
A tapestry, time's embrace.

Restful whispers, softly rise,
In this world of shifting skies.
Let the radiance guide your way,
Into the arms of the night's stay.

Sighs of the Midnight Breeze

Midnight sighs, a gentle breath,
Carrying tales of life and death.
Through the trees, it weaves and flows,
Kissing flowers, stirring prose.

Each whisper hunts for weary hearts,
In the stillness, a new start.
As shadows breathe the softest dreams,
The world unravels at its seams.

Winds caress, like lovers' hands,
Guiding souls to far-off lands.
A melody of calm persists,
In the night where magic twists.

With every sigh, the stars unwind,
Awakening the truths we find.
In the hush of midnight's ease,
We dance along with the breeze.

Celestial Nightscapes

Stars sprinkle across the black,
Painting dreams on a velvet track.
Galaxies spin in a cosmic lane,
Whispers lost in a stardust rain.

The moon, a guardian in the void,
Illuminates what fear destroyed.
Each twinkle tells of time and space,
In the universe's warm embrace.

Wonders vast, a sight to seek,
In celestial realms where silence speaks.
Here in the night, our spirits soar,
In nightscapes rich with ancient lore.

Eyes turned up, hearts aligned,
In the mystery, we find the signs.
A journey through the heavens wide,
In celestial nightscapes, we glide.

Shadows of Slumber

In whispers soft, the shadows creep,
They wrap the world in dreams so deep.
A tender hush, a gentle sigh,
As moonlit beams dance in the sky.

The night unveils its velvet cloak,
Where fantasies and hopes provoke.
In slumber's arms, we find our peace,
As time around us starts to cease.

Hidden realms within our minds,
In quietude, our heart unwinds.
The stars above, like diamonds bright,
Guide us through the sacred night.

So close your eyes, let worries fade,
Embrace the calm, the night's parade.
For in this dark, our spirits soar,
In shadows of slumber, we explore.

Imagining the Nightfall

When dusk arrives with colors rare,
The world transforms, beyond compare.
Each shadow lengthens, softly sprawled,
In twilight's grip, we are enthralled.

The painted sky, a deepening blue,
Whispers secrets, old yet new.
In silence, dreams begin to fray,
As night enfolds the fading day.

An orchestra of crickets sings,
While starlit glimmers, softly cling.
Imagining the nightfall's grace,
Where time slows down, and whispers trace.

With every heartbeat, magic calls,
In hushed embrace as twilight falls.
We find our place in night's embrace,
Imagining a dreamlike space.

Serene Echoes of Dusk

As daylight wanes, a hush prevails,
With gentle winds, the evening sails.
The golden rays begin to fade,
In serene echoes, life's parade.

Soft shadows blend with twilight's hue,
A canvas painted, fresh and new.
The chirps of birds, a lullaby,
In tranquil tones that softly sigh.

Along the horizon, colors blend,
A tapestry where day must end.
In twilight's arms, our worries cease,
In serene echoes, we find peace.

For every dusk brings night anew,
A promise stirred in every view.
So pause awhile, embrace the dusk,
In echoes soft, renew your trust.

Resting Under Starry Skies

Beneath the vault of starlit dreams,
We linger where the moonlight beams.
In tranquil whispers, night descends,
A cozy world where calm begins.

The galaxy paints a wondrous scene,
With constellations, bright and keen.
Each twinkle tells a tale of old,
A tapestry of dreams retold.

As cool winds brush against our skin,
The night unfolds from deep within.
Resting under a cosmic dome,
In starlit nights, we feel at home.

So breathe in deep this tranquil light,
Let go of all, embrace the night.
For in these moments, hearts align,
Under the stars, our souls entwine.

Basin of Moonlight

In the stillness of the night,
A basin filled with silver light.
Stars gather close, a secret choir,
Whispering dreams that never tire.

Soft waves crash on the shore,
Each moment asks for just one more.
Reflections dance on tranquil streams,
Cradled gently in our dreams.

Beneath the glow, the world feels right,
Wrapped in fabric woven tight.
Time suspended, hearts collide,
In this basin, we confide.

With every breath, the night begins,
A tapestry of all our sins.
Together here, we find our way,
In moonlit whispers, we will stay.

Sleeping Under Comet Trails

Under skies of endless flight,
We lay beneath the comet's light.
Wishes crafted on the breeze,
Carried off with gentle ease.

Stars parade in silent grace,
Each a story, each a face.
In the dark, our hopes ignite,
Burning bright through the night.

The cosmos sings a lullaby,
As we gaze up to the sky.
With dreams woven like a veil,
We are lost in comet trails.

In the heavens, echoes twine,
Our hearts beat in unison, divine.
Sleep now calls, our eyelids fall,
Beneath the comets, we have it all.

Comfort in the Quietude

In the hush of evening's sway,
Stars converse in their own way.
Soft whispers fill the air we share,
With each heartbeat, a tender prayer.

The world dissolves in shadows deep,
Crickets sing, and willows weep.
Finding solace, hand in hand,
In the quiet, we take a stand.

Every sigh is a sweet refrain,
Melodies of joy and pain.
Here amid the stillness we reside,
In the comfort of the quiet tide.

Wrapped in layers soft and warm,
We shelter close from any harm.
In this peace, our spirits soar,
Together always, forevermore.

Night's Cradle of Hush

Night descends with soft embrace,
A cradle in this tranquil space.
Beneath the stars, our secrets keep,
In the silence, we fall asleep.

Moonlight spills like liquid grace,
Painting shadows on our face.
Listen closely, the stillness sings,
Whispering tales of gentle things.

Wrapped in night's celestial shawl,
We feel the universe's call.
In this hushed and sacred place,
All our worries we erase.

As the world outside does fade,
Here in stillness, love is laid.
In night's cradle, dreams take flight,
Guided softly by the night.

Melodies of the Moonlit Sky

Whispers dance upon the breeze,
Silver beams through swaying trees.
Crickets sing their nightly tune,
Underneath the glowing moon.

Stars like gems in velvet spread,
Softly shining overhead.
Nature hums a soothing song,
Where the heart will soon belong.

Glistening rivers reflect light,
Carrying dreams into the night.
Every wave a gentle sigh,
Underneath the endless sky.

Lost in thoughts that gently flow,
In the night, our spirits grow.
Melodies that softly play,
Guide our souls till break of day.

Evening's Tender Caress

Shadows stretch as day concedes,
Night descends with gentle deeds.
Softly wraps the world in peace,
Bringing all our fears to cease.

Crimson fades to deep indigo,
Stars awaken, start to glow.
Moonlight traces paths of dreams,
In the quiet, comfort beams.

Breezes carry whispers sweet,
Nature's pulse with rhythm beat.
Every creature finds its place,
In the arms of night's embrace.

As we drift on softest sighs,
Underneath the velvet skies,
Evening wraps us all in grace,
Tenderly, the heart's embrace.

A Serenade for Sleep

Close your eyes and drift away,
Let the night softly sway.
Cradled in a silken dream,
Floating on a tranquil stream.

Rhythms of the heart align,
In the stillness, sweetly twine.
Lullabies that gently hum,
Promise rest will soon become.

Every sigh, a feathered breeze,
Carried forth on twilight seas.
In the hush, a story's spun,
Wrapped in warmth 'til night is done.

As the stars begin to gleam,
Slumber deepens like a dream.
A serenade, soft and sweet,
Guides us to the night's retreat.

Celestial Dreams Unfurled

In the hush of midnight's glow,
Whispers of the cosmos flow.
Dreams unfurl in tranquil light,
Taking wing into the night.

Constellations weave their tale,
Guiding hearts like ships with sail.
Nebulae of colors bright,
Paint the canvas of the night.

Time dissolves in starlit space,
Infinite, we find our place.
As we soar through skies of blue,
Dreams take flight, our spirits new.

Celestial visions call our name,
In the silence, spark the flame.
Together, reaching for the high,
In the space where dreams can fly.

Melodies of a Dreamer's Heart

Whispers float on the evening breeze,
Lost in thoughts, my spirit frees.
Each note dances, a gentle start,
Echoes soft in a dreamer's heart.

Under stars that softly gleam,
I wander deep in a silent dream.
With every sigh, a tale departs,
Carried on the wings of art.

The moonlight weaves through trees so tall,
Like silver threads, it binds us all.
In every shadow, a story parts,
Melodies sung by a dreamer's heart.

A Tapestry of Night's Comfort

In the stillness, night unfolds,
A blanket cast of silver gold.
Each star stitched in the velvet sky,
Where secrets whispered softly lie.

The world pauses, a gentle sigh,
Wrapped in darkness, dreams can fly.
Underneath this calming art,
We find our peace, a mother's heart.

Clouds drift slow like thoughts at play,
In this embrace, we find our way.
Night's comfort wraps like a soft dart,
Creating warmth in each heart.

The moon's gaze, a knowing spark,
Guiding souls that wander dark.
In this space, we are never apart,
Weaving dreams through night's art.

The Music of Closing Eyes

Each blink a note, a silent tune,
Under the watch of the gentle moon.
With closing eyes, the world retreats,
Melodies rise in soft heartbeats.

A symphony in shadows plays,
Whispers of night in soft ballet.
In the stillness, calmness lies,
Wrapped in the music of closing eyes.

Every sigh, a soft refrain,
Dancing lightly, free from pain.
A lullaby the heart now ties,
In the sweet music of closing eyes.

Drifting deeper, lost in bliss,
Each moment's end, a gentle kiss.
With every breath, serenity flies,
To the enchanting music of closing eyes.

Reflections on a Starry Canvas

A canvas stretches, vast and wide,
Stars like brushstrokes, side by side.
Each twinkle tells of dreams gone by,
Reflections dance in the silent sky.

Night's palette glows with hues untold,
Stories hidden in the bold.
In the silence, our wishes rise,
Reflections blooming in starry sighs.

As shadows play with glowing light,
We find our truths on this starry night.
The world below in peaceful guise,
Mirrors back through starry eyes.

Every heartbeat, a brush of chance,
Underneath this cosmic dance.
Capturing dreams where magic lies,
In reflections on a starry canvas.

Dreamweaver's Night

In shadows deep, the dreams do weave,
A tapestry of night, a soft reprieve.
Stars twinkle bright, guiding the way,
Through whispered thoughts where fantasies sway.

Luna's glow, a silent guide,
Cradles wishes that hearts confide.
With every blink, the visions soar,
Into realms unknown, forevermore.

The nightingale sings a wistful tune,
Under the watch of a silver moon.
In this embrace, we find our fate,
As dreamers dance, they vibrate.

So close your eyes, let slumber reign,
In dreamweaver's night, escape the pain.
Drift on clouds, where spirits play,
And hold the night till break of day.

The Moon's Sighing Secrets

The moon hangs low, a silent sage,
Whispering secrets on the night's stage.
Her silver beams cast gentle light,
Illuminating shadows with soft might.

Each sigh she takes, the stars align,
Guarding stories lost in time.
Celestial whispers fill the air,
Drawing dreams from hearts laid bare.

With every phase, her wisdom grows,
In her glow, a calming prose.
She speaks of love, of joy, of pain,
In night's embrace, all will remain.

Hear her sigh, listen close, my dear,
For in her breaths, the truth draws near.
A dance of light, a timeless waltz,
Unraveling mysteries, without faults.

Midnight Musings

In the stillness of the midnight hour,
Thoughts take flight, like a gentle flower.
Whispers of wonders brush the mind,
As fleeting moments, we seek to find.

Stars above, like dreams alive,
In slumber's grasp, our spirits thrive.
Ephemeral thoughts drift softly near,
A canvas painted, crystal clear.

Each flicker brings a tale untold,
Of love and loss, of dreams of gold.
Midnight musings, a sacred art,
Crafting stories from the heart.

Embrace the night, let shadows play,
In this quiet realm, we find our way.
For in these musings, we are free,
To chase the stars, eternally.

Slumber's Gracious Caress

Wrap me close in slumber's bliss,
A tranquil night, a gentle kiss.
With every breath, I drift away,
Into a world where dreams will stay.

The stars are seeds that softly bloom,
In the garden of my hidden room.
With every sigh, the night unfolds,
Stories whispered, secrets told.

Wrapped in warmth, I find my peace,
In slumber's arms, my thoughts release.
Endless fields of quiet grace,
In this embrace, I find my place.

So let the night take me away,
Where hope and dreams will gently sway.
In slumber's grasp, all fears express,
A sweet release, a soft caress.

Soft Shadows at Dusk

The sun dips low, the sky ablaze,
Soft shadows dance in twilight's haze.
Whispers of night begin to creep,
As the world prepares for sleep.

The trees stand tall, silhouettes cast,
Holding secrets of the past.
Crickets chirp a lullaby sweet,
A gentle tune where day and night meet.

Stars twinkle softly, one by one,
A canvas painted with the night's fun.
In this moment, time stands still,
A serene beauty, a quiet thrill.

Soft shadows linger, as dreams unfold,
In the magic of dusk, stories told.
With every breath, the night takes flight,
Embracing the peace of the coming night.

Whispering Breezes of Dusk

When daylight wanes, and colors blend,
A whispering breeze begins to send.
Messages from the evening sky,
Calling the stars, as they come nigh.

The rustling leaves tell tales of old,
Of secrets kept, and mysteries told.
In the gentle hush, the world sighs,
As the horizon kisses the cloudy skies.

Birds find rest in the branches wide,
While shadows deepen, and the night does bide.
Each breath of air, a soothing balm,
Wrapping the earth in a velvet calm.

In the twilight's grasp, we slowly blend,
With nature's rhythm, a perfect mend.
The whispering breezes embrace the dusk,
Crafting a moment, lovely and husk.

A Symphony for the Slumbering

The night unfolds a symphony sweet,
As stars begin their rhythmic beat.
With every note, the world calms down,
In a lullaby soft, the night wears a crown.

Moonlit melodies drift through the air,
Singing to dreams, both fragile and rare.
Each sigh a whisper, each heartbeat a song,
In this embrace, where we belong.

Crickets conduct from shadows deep,
While the world around begins to sleep.
The harmony wraps us, warm like a quilt,
In this serene place, where time is distilled.

Morning shall come, with its vibrant tune,
But for now, we sway beneath the moon.
A symphony for the slumbering sky,
In twilight's arms, we gently lie.

Ethereal Dreamscapes

In realms of night, where dreamers roam,
Ethereal dreamscapes feel like home.
A tapestry woven with starlit threads,
Where imagination flourishes and gently spreads.

Flight through clouds of silver and gold,
Whispers of stories yet to be told.
Figures dance in a fluid grace,
Lost in the magic of this sacred space.

Each vision glimmers, vivid and bright,
In the heart of the calm, enfolded by light.
Here, time flows like a gentle stream,
As we wander deep in a waking dream.

Ethereal whispers guide every thought,
In this haven of peace, solace is sought.
With stars as our lanterns, we choose our way,
In these dreamscapes, where we long to stay.

Star-Crossed Dreams

In the stillness of the night,
Wishes drift like fragile kites.
Beneath a tapestry of stars,
We chase the echoes of our hearts.

Whispers dance on lunar beams,
Carried soft on silver streams.
In secret corners of the mind,
We find the love we long to bind.

A fleeting glimpse, a gentle sigh,
Where love's sweet shadows never die.
In every heartbeat, dreams ignite,
A promise held in starlit flight.

These star-crossed dreams we dare to chase,
A cosmic waltz, a hidden place.
With every wish cast on night's dome,
We forge a path, we find our home.

A Blanket of Night Whispers

Cloaked in velvet, the night unfolds,
Secrets of the universe, told.
The gentle hush of twilight's breath,
Wraps around us, defying death.

Stars flicker softly, a mellow hum,
While shadows gather, quietly come.
In whispers shared, our dreams entwine,
Lost in the magic, feeling divine.

A blanket woven with threads of light,
Embraces us in the depth of night.
Together we sail on the milky way,
Through galaxies where lost souls play.

With every sigh, we weave new tales,
In the night's embrace, love never fails.
The whispers linger, sweet and clear,
In this blanket, we conquer fear.

Embracing the Shadowed Hours

In the twilight, shadows creep,
Where memories linger, soft and deep.
We wander through the dusky haze,
Embracing the night's tender gaze.

With every heartbeat, silence sings,
Echoes of laughter the darkness brings.
In moments stolen, time stands still,
Whispers of dreams we dare fulfill.

Together we dance in shadows cast,
A fleeting glimpse of futures past.
The moonlight guides our gentle fight,
Through the maze of the shadowed night.

We find our strength in the silent hours,
Blooming softly like midnight flowers.
With open hearts, between each star,
We embrace the night, no matter how far.

The Dusk Diary

In faded pages, secrets lay,
Captured moments, slipping away.
Each twilight holds a whispered tale,
Of dreams that wander, frail and pale.

With colors blending, day takes flight,
In the embrace of the quiet night.
Lines unbroken, yet words unsaid,
In the diary where hopes are fed.

The sun dips low, casting its glow,
Ink of the sky begins to flow.
Every shadow, a story spun,
In the dusk's embrace, our hearts rerun.

We write our fables on the breeze,
Pages turning with every tease.
In the dusk diary, our souls unite,
Finding solace in the fading light.

Moonlit Serenades

Underneath the silver glow,
Whispers dance on evening's breeze,
Songs of love and sweet hello,
Carried softly through the trees.

Stars above in quiet tune,
Guide the night with gentle light,
As we sway beneath the moon,
Hearts ignited, pure delight.

Laughter mingles with the night,
Echoes of a time so sweet,
In this dream, our souls take flight,
Moonlit paths where lovers meet.

Dreams in Silver Whispers

In the stillness, dreams arise,
Silver whispers, soft and clear,
Fluttering like ancient sighs,
Carried forth to hold us near.

Fleeting moments slip away,
Glimmers of a future bright,
In the night, our hopes can play,
Wrapped in warmth, a soft twilight.

Each breath held a secret key,
Unlocking worlds unseen, unknown,
In this realm, just you and me,
Where the seeds of love are sown.

Night's Gentle Embrace

Wrapped in shadows, soft and deep,
Night unfolds her tender grace,
Cradling all who wish to sleep,
In the silence, find your place.

Stars above, like diamonds bright,
Glimmer softly through the haze,
Guiding dreams within the night,
In their warmth, our spirits gaze.

Every heartbeat sings of peace,
As the world outside grows still,
Here beneath the night's release,
Hope and solace gently fill.

Stardust Slumber

Beneath the veil of twilight skies,
Magic stirs in quiet grace,
Wrapped in stardust lullabies,
In this sacred, peaceful space.

Softly drifting into dreams,
Where reality softly fades,
Riding on the moon's bright beams,
In a dance that never wades.

Every wish a starry spark,
Guiding us through endless nights,
In the realm where visions mark,
Heartfelt joys and pure delights.

Serenading the Sleepy Stars

In the twilight's gentle hush,
Stars begin their nightly rush.
Whispers float on velvet air,
Dreams emerge, both light and rare.

Crickets chirp in soft refrain,
As moonbeams dance on windowpanes.
Nights ignite with silver spark,
Guiding souls through velvet dark.

Each twinkle tells a story bright,
Wrapped in mystery and light.
The cosmos sings a lullaby,
To weary hearts as they sigh.

So let the night embrace our quest,
With starlit dreams, we find our rest.

Crickets' Nighttime Melody

In fields where shadows softly creep,
Crickets chirp while the world sleeps.
Their chorus weaves a tapestry,
Of nature's sweet simplicity.

Flickering fireflies light the way,
As twilight turns to gentle gray.
Nature's song in the chilling breeze,
Brings hearts to rest with graceful ease.

The harmony of night unfolds,
In stories whispered, yet untold.
Crickets play their timeless role,
Igniting peace within the soul.

So close your eyes and hear their call,
Embrace the night, let worries fall.

Pillows of Celestial Light

Underneath the starlit dome,
We find a world that feels like home.
Pillows filled with dreams so bright,
Cradle hopes in soft moonlight.

Clouds drift by like whispers soft,
Carrying wishes, let them loft.
In slumber deep, our spirits soar,
Touched by light forevermore.

Each star a beacon, shining clear,
Guiding lost hearts, holding near.
In this realm of endless night,
We grasp the gleam of purest light.

Rest your head, let worries cease,
In this quiet, find your peace.

A Nocturnal Nurturing

As night unfolds its tender care,
Soft winds whisper secrets rare.
Leaves rustle in a rhythmic sway,
Embracing dreams till break of day.

The moon's glow bathes the earth in gold,
Boundless tales waiting to be told.
Creatures dwell in shadows deep,
In their world, the magic sleeps.

Stars ignite with a soothing grace,
Cradling dreams in their embrace.
In the quiet, hearts will mend,
A night of healing without end.

Close your eyes, surrender plight,
To the magic of the night.

Enchanted Dreams Await

In whispers soft, the night unfolds,
Where silent secrets softly told.
With ivy vines and moonlit beams,
The magic stirs in distant dreams.

Beneath the stars, the shadows play,
As night transforms the dusk to day.
In slumber's grasp, the heart takes flight,
To realms unknown, in purest light.

On velvet wings, the visions soar,
Through glittering skies, forevermore.
As dreams entwine, their tales ignite,
The promise of a new dawn's light.

Mysteries of the Midnight Hour

The clock strikes twelve, the world falls still,
In every heart, a whispered thrill.
Shadows dance where secrets creep,
In midnight's grasp, the dreamers leap.

Voices echo in the night,
Guiding lost souls toward the light.
With every breath, the mysteries call,
As hidden truths begin to sprawl.

Through tangled paths and starlit skies,
The unseen world begins to rise.
In realms where logic fades away,
The midnight hour holds its sway.

The Shadowed Canvas

A canvas stretched in shades of gray,
Where dreams and fears collide and play.
With gentle strokes, the brush begins,
To paint the stories deep within.

Each line a whisper, soft and bold,
In colors rare, both bright and cold.
The shadows breathe, the light retreats,
In every hue, the heart competes.

Emotions swirl in darkened tones,
Revealing depths, the soul atones.
A masterpiece of pain and grace,
The shadowed canvas holds its place.

Starry Night's Embrace

The sky adorned with glimmering light,
As gentle stars greet the night.
In endless dance, they twinkle bright,
A constellation of pure delight.

Embraced by dreams, the world unwinds,
With cosmic whispers, love rebinds.
In silent awe, we gaze above,
Amidst the wishes, fate and love.

The night unfolds its velvet charm,
In every shimmer, a gentle balm.
Together lost in starlit grace,
We find our place in night's embrace.

Slumber's Sweet Song

Close your eyes, let dreams take flight,
Whispers soft in the still of night.
Stars above blink in delight,
Cradling hopes till morning light.

Gentle waves of the night's embrace,
Lull your cares, in this sacred space.
Let the calmness slow your pace,
In slumber's arms, find your place.

Moonlight dances on your skin,
Softly guiding where dreams begin.
In this world, let joy seep in,
Awake to love, where hearts have been.

Awash in twilight's glowing seam,
Life transforms into a dream.
Caught in hope's tender beam,
Sleep tonight, your soul shall gleam.

Cosmic Cradles

In the cradle of the night,
Stars assemble, pure and bright.
Galaxies spin, worlds delight,
Whispering secrets, pure and light.

Cosmic winds begin to sing,
Carrying tales of everything.
Nebulas in a vibrant ring,
Unfolding wonders that time can bring.

Shooting stars, your wishes fly,
Across the canvas of the sky.
In quiet moments, hear the sigh,
Of dreams that once dared to try.

Cradled in celestial grace,
Hearts beat in this endless space.
In the vastness, we find our place,
Linked through time, a shared embrace.

Echoes of the Quiet Dark

In shadows deep, silence reigns,
Where secrets hide, and stillness gains.
Echoes whisper soft refrains,
In quiet dark, where peace remains.

The moon bestows its silver hue,
Casting dreams in shades anew.
Every heartbeat echoes true,
In soft repose, a tranquil view.

Shadows stretch, the night unfolds,
Stories whispered, tales retold.
In the dark, we find the bold,
In shadows' embrace, hearts consoled.

A symphony of crisp night air,
Wraps the world, in wonders rare.
Each echo tells us it's so fair,
In quiet dark, love's always there.

Harmonies of the Night Breeze

Breezes weave through branches sigh,
Carrying dreams, whispering by.
In nature's rhythm, hearts comply,
Dancing softly beneath the sky.

Gentle rustle, leaves' sweet song,
In the night where we belong.
Life's gentle pulse, where souls are strong,
Harmonies weave, the night's lifelong.

Stars twinkle in the clear, cool air,
Breath of night, soothing and rare.
Embrace the peace, shed every care,
In the magic of twilight's glare.

In its embrace, we find our muse,
Night's soft breath, we shall not lose.
With every note, the heart renews,
In the breeze, the night softly cues.

Nocturnal Requiem

In shadows deep where whispers dwell,
The night unfolds its silent spell.
Stars like lanterns softly gleam,
While dreams dissolve in twilight's seam.

A haunting song upon the breeze,
Carries tales of forgotten pleas.
The moon, a witness, brave and bold,
Keeps secrets safe from ages old.

Awake, the ghosts of yesteryears,
They dance with echoes, spark our fears.
Yet in the dark, a beauty lingers,
As fate weaves tales with gentle fingers.

Beneath the veil of starry light,
Restless souls embrace the night.
In peace they find their solemn home,
Within the shadows, free to roam.

Celestial Cradles

In the arms of cosmic grace,
Stars like children find their place.
Galaxies in twinkling play,
Cradle dreams of night and day.

Whispers of the stardust rare,
Fill the void with gentle care.
Comets sweep through velvet skies,
Painting trails where hope relies.

Nebulas in colors bright,
Dance and spin in sheer delight.
Each embrace, a timeless song,
In this cradle, we belong.

As planets spin in vast array,
Destinies entwine and sway.
In this cosmic lullaby,
Wonders bloom and never die.

Twilight's Tender Songs

In twilight's glow, the whispers rise,
A serenade beneath soft skies.
Colors blend in warm embrace,
As daylight bows, it leaves a trace.

Song of crickets, sweetly played,
Notes that weave through glades, delayed.
The rustle of the leaves, a hymn,
As twilight's veil grows soft and dim.

Fireflies flicker, lanterns bright,
Guiding dreams into the night.
A lullaby of dusk unfolds,
As twilight's tender heart beholds.

In this hour, time stands still,
Nature's pulse, a soothing thrill.
We close our eyes, surrender deep,
To twilight's songs, in peace we sleep.

Serenity of the Moon's Gaze

Beneath the moon's serene embrace,
The world finds calm, a tranquil space.
Silvery beams kiss the night,
Illuminating paths of light.

In stillness deep, the heart can rest,
Wrapped in dreams, the soul is blessed.
The nightingale sings soft and low,
In harmony with moonlit glow.

Time drifts slowly, moments fleet,
As gentle whispers float and meet.
Each breath a balm, a soothing balm,
In the moon's gaze, everything's calm.

A tapestry of stars unfold,
Stories of the brave and bold.
We wander 'neath the silver gleam,
Embracing peace, forever dream.

A Soothing Serenade to the Moon

In silver light, the world stands still,
Whispers of night, a gentle thrill.
Stars twinkle softly, secrets unfold,
Dreams painted bright, in hues of gold.

The nightingale sings, sweet lullabies,
Beneath the glow of starry skies.
Moonbeams dance on the tranquil sea,
Inviting hearts to be wild and free.

In this embrace, all worries cease,
A perfect moment, purest peace.
Bathed in light, a world reborn,
In moonlit dreams, we are adorned.

So let us wander, hand in hand,
Through silver fields, across the land.
With every sigh, the night unfolds,
A soothing serenade, forever told.

Nighttime Tales and Fables

Under the cloak of a starry night,
Whispers of stories take their flight.
Wolves howl softly, the owls agree,
Nature's chorus sings wild and free.

Tales of old dance in the air,
Of brave knights and maidens fair.
Moonlit castles in shadows loom,
While fireflies weave through the darkened gloom.

Fables of courage, love, and woe,
Echo in silence, soft and slow.
A flicker of magic, tales unfold,
In every heart, a story told.

So gather round, let dreams ignite,
In the embrace of a cozy night.
For every star, a story shines,
In nighttime fables, our hope aligns.

The Pulse of Midnight Hearts

Beneath the blanket of midnight skies,
The pulse of hearts beats low and wise.
Each throb a whisper, a hidden quest,
In the stillness, dreams find rest.

Shadows dance on the wall so bright,
Counting moments in the hush of night.
With every heartbeat, memories swirl,
In the sacred calm, our hopes unfurl.

Rivers of silence flow deep and wide,
As secrets of souls in the shadows abide.
The universe listens, tender and true,
In this heartbeat, I'm lost in you.

So let us linger, in this embrace,
Where love writes time at its own pace.
Together we form a timeless art,
Bound forever by the pulse of hearts.

The Poetry of Night's Silence

In the hush of night, stars gleam bright,
Whispers of dreams take their flight,
Moonlit shadows dance with grace,
In this tranquility, we find our place.

Luminous tales from the skies,
Softly told in starlit sighs,
Each moment cloaked in deep repose,
In silence, the heart truly knows.

The world outside sleeps in peace,
Where all worries find their cease,
Time slows down, as if to say,
Night's silence holds the fears at bay.

In this calm, let your soul flow,
With every breath, let love grow,
Under the blanket of the night,
We find our dreams take sudden flight.

Snoozing under Cosmic Canopies

Boundless skies with stars aglow,
Wrapped in warmth, we breathe in slow,
Dreams drift softly like clouds above,
In cosmic realms, we find our love.

Galaxies swirl in a dance divine,
While heartbeats sync with space and time,
Restful minds traverse the void,
In stillness, all chaos is destroyed.

Nebulas bloom in colors bright,
As we cuddle in the velvet night,
A tapestry of dreams unfolds,
In cosmic arms, forever holds.

With the universe, we become one,
A gentle lullaby has begun,
Sleep beneath the stardust's gaze,
In dreamland, we spend our days.

Wavelengths of Wonderment

Ripples of thought in the silent air,
Vibrations of joy, beyond compare,
In every pulse, a story is spun,
Wavelengths of wonder, we've just begun.

Feel the rhythm of hearts in sync,
Each beat a note, as dreams interlink,
In the dance of life, we soar and sway,
Melodies of hope light up the way.

Colors collide in a dazzling show,
As ideas blossom, together we grow,
In this moment, creation's muse,
We ride the waves, we cannot lose.

Follow the whispers of dreams untold,
In the spectrum of life, be brave and bold,
Embrace the wavelengths, let them extend,
In the heart of wonder, we find our end.

The Garden of Dreams

In the garden where wishes bloom,
Magic lingers, dispelling gloom,
Petals of hope in colors bright,
Whispering secrets of pure delight.

Paths of starlight lead us near,
To buds of laughter, void of fear,
Each fragrant breath, a world so wide,
In this haven, let dreams reside.

Trees of wisdom, roots held tight,
Branches reaching to the light,
In this sanctuary, dreams take flight,
Filling the air with pure delight.

Dance within this vibrant space,
In the garden of dreams, find your place,
With every heartbeat, let it seem,
Together we weave the thread of dream.

The Nightingale's Softest Song

In shadows deep, the nightingale sings,
A melody that softly clings.
With every note, the silence breaks,
In whispered tones, the heart awakes.

Beneath the stars, her voice does soar,
A serenade forevermore.
The moonlight dances on the leaves,
As nature listens, and believes.

Each fluttered wing, a tale unfolds,
In gentle rhymes, her story told.
Her song, a balm for weary souls,
In twilight's breath, the magic rolls.

So in the night, let dreams take flight,
With nightingale, we find our light.
In every verse, a heart's delight,
As all the world holds still, and tight.

Moonshine and Mellow Moments

The moonlight casts a silver glow,
On tranquil streams, where soft winds blow.
In quiet laughter shared so sweet,
Time drifts like whispers at our feet.

Mellow moments fill the air,
As stars above begin to flare.
We sip the joy, we taste the night,
In every glance, the hearts take flight.

The world feels still, the night divine,
In every sigh, your hand in mine.
With each soft word, the shadows play,
A symphony that leads the way.

In moonshine's glow, we dream and weave,
Our memories, a quilt to leave.
In quiet charms, forever hold,
These moments, cherished, and retold.

Driftwood Thoughts Under A Starlit Sky

Upon the shore, the driftwood lies,
Beneath the vast and starlit skies.
Each piece a story, lost at sea,
In whispered dreams, they speak to me.

The ocean hums a gentle tune,
While night embraces the silver moon.
I ponder life's mysterious art,
As driftwood thoughts entwine my heart.

The winds whisper secrets of the deep,
In shadows where the silence sleeps.
Beneath the stars, I find my place,
In nature's arms, a warm embrace.

Each grain of sand, each wave that swells,
Holds stories, echoes, ancient bells.
With driftwood thoughts that gently sigh,
I drift and dream, beneath the sky.

Whispers of the Sleeping Earth

In twilight's hush, the earth does breathe,
A silent promise, soft and grieved.
Beneath the soil, life stirs and sighs,
In whispers carried through the skies.

The roots entwine in dark embrace,
While shadows flicker, leaving trace.
With every rustle, secrets spill,
In nature's realm, our spirits fill.

The sleeping earth, a world concealed,
In dreams of green, the heart is healed.
With every pulse, a heartbeat wild,
In whispered songs, we are beguiled.

So let us rest, in silence found,
Among the whispers, all around.
For in this peace, our souls will mend,
In quiet grace, we find our friend.

Secrets Beneath the Moon

Whispers dance on silver beams,
Hidden tales of silent dreams.
In shadows deep, the secrets sway,
Beneath the moon's soft, gentle ray.

Ancient whispers call my name,
In the night, they stoke the flame.
A beckoning to stars above,
In this silence, I find love.

Through the mist, the stories gleam,
Carried on the wind's sweet dream.
The night holds a magic spell,
In its arms, I wish to dwell.

Moonlit paths I gladly roam,
Finding comfort, finding home.
Secrets linger close and near,
Underneath the moonlit sphere.

A Voyage of Dream Clouds

Sailing high on wispy dreams,
Floating softly, it seems.
In the skies, where hopes align,
Journey whispers, pure and fine.

Each cloud a story waiting there,
Carried gently in the air.
Drifting through a world of thought,
In this realm, my dreams are caught.

Colors swirl in endless flight,
Painting visions, bold and bright.
On this voyage, time stands still,
Chasing dreams with steadfast will.

Beneath the stars, my spirit sings,
As the night its solace brings.
A tapestry of dreams unfurled,
In this vast, enchanting world.

Twilight's Soothing Embrace

Gentle glow of twilight's hue,
Wraps the world in shades of blue.
As the day begins to fade,
Evening whispers softly made.

Birds retreat to nest in rest,
Nature sighs, her heart confessed.
In the calm, the shadows play,
As light bids the sun away.

Stars awaken, one by one,
In the cradle of the sun.
Twilight holds a tender grace,
In her soothing, warm embrace.

Embers of the day are gone,
As night draws its velvet lawn.
In this stillness, I find peace,
In twilight's love, all troubles cease.

The Stillness Between Stars

In the void, where silence sings,
Darkness wraps its fragile wings.
Between each star, a breath is drawn,
In the night, the dreams are born.

Galaxies hold whispers near,
In their light, I feel no fear.
Time suspended, gently sways,
Holding secrets of the days.

Every flicker tells a tale,
In the dark, where wishes sail.
The cosmos hums a timeless song,
In this stillness, I belong.

Boundless reaches stretch and flow,
In the night, my spirit knows.
Amid the silence, I will find,
A universe within my mind.

Starlit Lull

The night whispers soft and low,
Beneath the stars' gentle glow.
Dreams dance in the moon's embrace,
In a tranquil, velvet space.

Crickets sing a soothing tune,
As silver beams kiss the dune.
Rest your weary, wandering mind,
In this haven, peace you'll find.

The world drifts away, so far,
In the light of a guiding star.
Let your thoughts gently wane,
Wrapped in night's sweet refrain.

As shadows weave through the trees,
Lullabies ride on the breeze.
Close your eyes, let dreams take flight,
In the calm of this starlit night.

Embrace of the Quiet Sky

The sky unfolds, a blanket wide,
Where the moon and stars abide.
Whispers float on twilight air,
In this moment, nothing's rare.

Cradled by the night's soft sigh,
We let go of time gone by.
Stars embrace us, shining bright,
Guiding souls through velvet night.

With every twinkle, hope is spun,
Dreams awaken, one by one.
In the stillness, hearts connect,
Underneath this vast, sweet sect.

The canvas dark, yet full of light,
Painting shadows, chasing fright.
In the calm, our spirits rise,
In the embrace of quiet skies.

Nocturne of the Dreaming Hearts

In dusk's arms, the day departs,
Awakening the dreaming hearts.
Underneath the starry dome,
We find love, we find our home.

The world fades, a gentle sigh,
As moonbeams weave a lullaby.
Whispers soft like a breeze,
Kiss our thoughts, bring us ease.

With every pulse of night's sweet grace,
The universe holds us in its embrace.
A symphony of dreams takes flight,
In the magic of the night.

Lost in wonder, free of fears,
We dance lightly through the years.
Nocturne plays, our hearts entwine,
In the glow of love divine.

Silken Shadows

In the hush where shadows lie,
Whispers fade and moments sigh.
Silken threads of night unfurl,
Creating dreams that gently swirl.

A tapestry of calm surrounds,
Where the stillness softly sounds.
Gentle breezes brush the trees,
In this world, we find our ease.

With every flicker of the stars,
Our worries drift, erased by Mars.
In the depth of twilight's glow,
Secrets of the heart we show.

Silken shadows cradle night,
Guiding lost souls to the light.
With every heartbeat, we are drawn,
To the magic of the dawn.

Starlit Dreams

In the night, dreams softly gleam,
Sparkling like a quiet stream.
Woven tales of hope and grace,
Bloom beneath the starry face.

Find your peace in twilight's arms,
Wrapped in night's enchanting charms.
Let your spirit roam and play,
In the starlit dance of day.

Guided by the moon's sweet beam,
We embrace the night's soft dream.
Whispers echo, hearts align,
In the tapestry divine.

Sleep now, child of light and lore,
Tomorrow brings you even more.
In starlit dreams, we find our way,
Guided gently towards the day.

Twilight's Embrace of Peace

The sun dips low, a fading light,
Soft shadows dance, embracing night.
Whispers of calm in the gentle breeze,
Nature's lullaby, a sweet reprise.

Stars peek out, in velvet skies,
A canvas painted with soft sighs.
Time slows down in this tranquil hour,
A moment held, a fleeting power.

The world's heartbeat, slow and sweet,
Each pulse a promise, a soft retreat.
In twilight's arms, we find our place,
Wrapped in warmth, a tender grace.

As darkness falls, the dreams ignite,
In twilight's embrace, all feels right.
A peaceful heart, a peaceful mind,
In every corner, solace we find.

The Rhythm of Nightfall

Night descends with whispers low,
A secret dance, a soft glow.
Stars take their positions high,
As the moon begins to sigh.

The world relents, its worries cease,
In the darkness, we find peace.
Crickets play their evening song,
While the shadows stretch along.

Each heartbeat syncs with nighttime's pulse,
As velvet night begins to convulse.
The air is thick with dreams untold,
In this rhythm, we feel bold.

With every sigh, the night unfolds,
Sweet stories shared, and secrets told.
In the hush, we hear the call,
The rhythm of nightfall, embracing all.

Moonlit Whispers

Underneath the silver moon,
Whispers dance, a soft tune.
Shadows play on fields of light,
Embracing dreams deep in the night.

A gentle breeze stirs the trees,
Carrying tales upon the seas.
Stars twinkle in a cosmic ballet,
Guiding our hearts on this journey's way.

The world transforms in shades of blue,
With every glance, there's something new.
In moonlit paths, we wander free,
Lost in whispers, just you and me.

Together we share this magic hour,
Wrapped in the moon's ethereal power.
With each heartbeat, love's secrets flow,
In the silence, our souls softly glow.

Celestial Serenades

Stars compose their lullabies,
In cosmic realms, where silence lies.
Each twinkle holds a story rare,
Celestial serenades in the air.

Galaxies spin in graceful arcs,
Painting dreams with gentle sparks.
In this vast expanse, we find our place,
Embraced by the night's warm embrace.

Comets trace their fleeting trails,
While moonlight weaves enchanting tales.
The universe hums a timeless song,
In celestial realms, we all belong.

As night unfolds its tapestry,
We dance in rhythm, wild and free.
With every note in this starlit space,
Celestial serenades light our chase.

Shimmering Dreams on Velvet Nights

Underneath the stars so bright,
Whispers linger, taking flight.
Softly glimmers, silver beams,
In the silence, dance of dreams.

Velvet skies embrace the night,
Heartbeats match the soft moonlight.
Every shadow, gentle grace,
In this realm, we find our place.

Lullabies of crickets play,
Guiding thoughts that drift away.
In the calm, our wishes gleam,
We awaken to the dream.

Hold the magic, soft and dear,
In these moments, free of fear.
Shimmer bright, our hopes in sight,
On velvet nights, we take our flight.

The Stillness of Midnight

In the stillness, time stands still,
A quiet heart, a whispered thrill.
Moonlit paths, where shadows blend,
Embrace the night, let worries end.

Each breath echoes, a silent song,
In the darkness, we belong.
Stars above like diamonds shine,
In this moment, all is fine.

Fleeting thoughts drift through the air,
All my secrets laid bare.
Wrapped in stillness, feel the grace,
In midnight's arms, we find our place.

Dreams awaken, softly spun,
In the hush, we are as one.
Time moves gently, a tender guide,
In the stillness, love won't hide.

Nighttime's Gentle Tides

Waves of velvet wash ashore,
Each heartbeat, a whispered lore.
Moonlit shimmer on the sea,
Guiding souls to be set free.

Gentle breezes kiss the waves,
Whispers hush, the night behaves.
Stars align, a dance so true,
In this moment, just me and you.

Rhythms pulse, the tides awake,
Breath of night, the world we make.
Softly crashing, a lullaby,
In evening's arms, we softly sigh.

Lost in time, we drift along,
In the still, we hear the song.
Nighttime's gentle tides bestow,
Endless dreams to ebb and flow.

Serenade of the Sleeping Moon

Underneath the silver glow,
Whispers of the night bestow.
Crickets sing a soft refrain,
In the quiet, peace remains.

Moonlight dances on the trees,
With the breeze, a sighing tease.
Dreams awakened, softly spun,
In the serenade, we're one.

Stars are listening, hearts in sync,
What we feel, in thoughts we think.
As the night wraps us in bliss,
Every moment holds a kiss.

Sleepy eyes and tender sighs,
In this dream, love never dies.
Serenade of the moon so bright,
Guides us gently through the night.

Milton Keynes UK
Ingram Content Group UK Ltd.
UKHW021127021124
450571UK00005B/72

9 789916 903643